ISBN 978-0-266-80304-1
PIBN 10891844

Canadian Institute for Historical Microreproductions / Institut canadien de microreproductions historiques

may be bibliographically unique, which may alter any of the images in the reproduction, or which may significantly change the usual method of filming, are checked below.

exemplaire qui sont peut-être uniques du point de vue bibliographique, qui peuvent modifier une image reproduite, ou qui peuvent exiger une modification dans la méthode normale de filmage sont indiqués ci-dessous.

☑ Coloured covers/
Couverture de couleur

☑ Covers damaged/
Couverture endommagée

☐ Covers restored and/or laminated/
Couverture restaurée et/ou pelliculée

☐ Cover title missing/
Le titre de couverture manque

☐ Coloured maps/
Cartes géographiques en couleur

☑ Coloured ink (i.e. other than blue or black)/
Encre de couleur (i.e. autre que bleue ou noire)

☐ Coloured plates and/or illustrations/
Planches et/ou illustrations en couleur

☐ Bound with other material/
Relié avec d'autres documents

☐ Tight binding may cause shadows or distortion along interior margin/
La reliure serrée peut causer de l'ombre ou de la distorsion le long de la marge intérieure

☐ Blank leaves added during restoration may appear within the text. Whenever possible, these have been omitted from filming/
Il se peut que certaines pages blanches ajoutées lors d'une restauration apparaissent dans le texte, mais, lorsque cela était possible, ces pages n'ont pas été filmées.

☑ Additional comments:/
Commentaires supplémentaires:

☑ Coloured pages/
Pages de couleur

☑ Pages damaged/
Pages endommagées

☐ Pages restored and/or laminated/
Pages restaurées et/ou pelliculées

☑ Pages discoloured, stained or foxed/
Pages décolorées, tachetées ou piquées

☐ Pages detached/
Pages détachées

☑ Showthrough/
Transparence

☑ Quality of print varies/
Qualité inégale de l'impression

☐ Continuous pagination/
Pagination continue

☐ Includes index(es)/
Comprend un (des) index

Title on header taken from:/
Le titre de l'en-tête provient:

☐ Title page of issue/
Page de titre de la livraison

☐ Caption of issue/
Titre de départ de la livraison

☐ Masthead/
Générique (périodiques) de la livraison

Printed announcement tipped in.

This item is filmed at the reduction ratio checked below/
Ce document est filmé au taux de réduction indiqué ci-dessous.

The images appearing here are the best quality possible considering the condition and legibility of the original copy and in keeping with the filming contract specifications.

Original copies in printed paper covers are filmed beginning with the front cover and ending on the last page with a printed or illustrated impression, or the back cover when appropriate. All other original copies are filmed beginning on the first page with a printed or illustrated impression, and ending on the last page with a printed or illustrated impression.

The last recorded frame on each microfiche shall contain the symbol ➞ (meaning "CONTINUED"), or the symbol ▽ (meaning "END"), whichever applies.

Maps, plates, charts, etc., may be filmed at different reduction ratios. Those too large to be entirely included in one exposure are filmed beginning in the upper left hand corner, left to right and top to bottom, as many frames as required. The following diagrams illustrate the method:

Les images suivantes ont été reproduites avec le plus grand soin, compte tenu de la condition et de la netteté de l'exemplaire filmé, et en conformité avec les conditions du contrat de filmage.

Les exemplaires originaux dont la couverture en papier est imprimée sont filmés en commençant par le premier plat et en terminant soit par la dernière page qui comporte une empreinte d'impression ou d'illustration, soit par le second plat, selon le cas. Tous les autres exemplaires originaux sont filmés en commençant par la première page qui comporte une empreinte d'impression ou d'illustration et en terminant par la dernière page qui comporte une telle empreinte.

Un des symboles suivants apparaîtra sur la dernière image de chaque microfiche, selon le cas: le symbole ➞ signifie "A SUIVRE", le symbole ▽ signifie "FIN".

Les cartes, planches, tableaux, etc., peuvent être filmés à des taux de réduction différents. Lorsque le document est trop grand pour être reproduit en un seul cliché, il est filmé à partir de l'angle supérieur gauche, de gauche à droite, et de haut en bas, en prenant le nombre d'images nécessaire. Les diagrammes suivants illustrent la méthode.

| 1 | 2 | 3 |

| 1 |
| 2 |
| 3 |

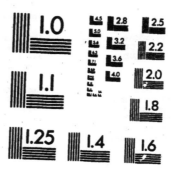

On The MAKING of BLANK-BOOKS.

Printing
Announcement

Warwick
~~~ ~~~ers
and
Rutter

68, 70 Front
Street West
Toronto •
Canada

ESSRS. WARWICK BROTHERS AND
RUTTER TAKE PLEASURE IN
FURTHER INTRODUCING THEIR
LARGE AND WELL-EQUIPPED
FACTORY TO THEIR FRIENDS AND
CUSTOMERS · IN ADDITION TO THE MANUFAC-
TURE OF BLANK BOOKS, WHICH IS DESCRIBED
IN DETAIL IN THE ACCOMPANYING BOOKLET,
THE PRINTING OF BOOKS, CATALOGUES AND
BOOKLETS IS AN INCREASINGLY LARGE AND
IMPORTANT PART OF THEIR BUSINESS · THEIR
PRINTING DEPARTMENT IS FURNISHED WITH
THE MOST MODERN APPLIANCES FOR THE PRO-
DUCTION OF FINE BOOKS, AND ALL WORK
ENTRUSTED TO THEM IS EXECUTED IN THE
BEST STYLE OF THE PRINTER'S ART . . . . . .

BUSINESS MEN WHO CONTEMPLATE ISSUING
CATALOGUES OR BOOKLETS OF ANY KIND WILL
FIND IT OF ADVANTAGE TO CONSULT THEM
REGARDING STYLE AND ARRANGEMENT . . . .

ADDRESS 68 AND 70 FRONT STREET WEST,
TORONTO.

WARWICK BRO'S & RUTTER

WAREHOUSE AND FACTORY

On the Making of Blank-Books

ȝ

ISSUED BY WARWICK BRO'S AND
RUTTER, STATIONERS, PRINTERS,
BOOKBINDERS AND MANUFACTURERS
OF BLANK-BOOKS, 68 AND 70 FRONT
STREET WEST TORONTO . . . .

" We desire, since it costs no more in time or trouble, to create first-class artisans . . . The book, not only essentially, but as a whole, is far from being an ordinary object. . . . He who is entrusted with encasing and embellishing it should possess good taste and be capable of understanding its requirements. Even the powers of an artist are not beyond this delicate work—a work more difficult than is generally thought. It is to this end that we . . . instruct the youth who are to engage in the industry of book-binding."

On The
MAKING
of BLANK-BOOKS

OOKMAKING, which, to-day, has reached almost the ideal of perfection, had its beginning in the crude efforts of the early writers to fasten together the sheets of bark, metal or parchment upon which they had cut or written their records. The modern word "book" is derived from the old Saxon word "boc," or "beech," indicating that the early writing was inscribed on boards or bark cut from beech trees. The binder's work at that time consisted in securing the different pieces with clamps or hinges, or with cords passed through a hole in the corner of the blocks. During the middle ages, and down to the invention of printing, bookmaking was entirely in the hands of the professional copyists in the different monasteries, whose work consisted in transcribing and ornamenting old Latin manuscripts for the use of the monks or for wealthy laymen ambitious of collecting a library. The duty of the binder was to sew together the different pieces on rawhide bands, and to encase them in wooden boards with an outer covering of leather or velvet. The covering was then decorated with a fanciful design burnt into the surface by heated tools, similar in character to those used by modern book-finishers.

The result of the introduction of printing was a vast increase in the production of books, and many improvements have been made in the art of bookmaking since that time. These, however, have been mainly in a greater perfection of workmanship and in the use of finer and better materials ; for books to-day are bound substantially as they were in the fifteenth and sixteenth centuries.

The art of bookbinding is now divided into two distinct branches : letterpress binding and blank-book binding. Speaking generally, all books consisting of reading matter are classed as letterpress books, and all others, whether plain, ruled or printed, are called blank-books. The work of the letterpress and the blank-book binders is totally different, and few workmen have a thorough knowledge of both branches. The development of large binderies, or bookmaking factories, has resulted in workmen becoming specialists in different branches of the trade, rather than bookbinders in the true sense of the word ; and as the whole thought and attention of each workman are given to his own branch, whether as ruler, sewer, marbler, cutter, forwarder or finisher, the books produced to-day are neater, and stronger, and better than ever before.

BOOKBINDING

The paper which enters into the making of blank-books varies according to the size and character of the book. For the smaller and cheaper books paper is made in a score of qualities and in as many weights ; but foolscap, small post, large post, and double foolscap, are the sizes mainly employed. For the larger books the finest of linen ledger and hand-made papers only are used. These are made of strong fibrous materials, capable of withstanding the heavy wear and tear to which such books are subjected. These papers are specially suited to bear

PAPER

Royal -	-	-	-	19 x 24	44
Super Royal	-	-		20 x 28	54
Imperial	-	-	-	23 x 31	72

If larger books are required, certain of these papers may be had in double sizes, as double foolscap, double demy, double medium, and for smaller ones the papers may be cut or folded in any way desired.

A blank-book, in the course of manufacture, passes through many hands. Except for ruling and trimming, machinery has no part in its making. It is entirely a hand-made article. Skill knowledge and judgment are the essential qualifications in a good bookbinder. He alone is responsible for the strength and stability, the shape and set of the book. He selects the proper boards and the most suitable piece of leather for each individual book. He must know when to act and how. The shape of the back, the setting of the glue, the stretching of the leather, are matters of the utmost importance, and no two books even of the same size, but of different thickness, are bound exactly alike.

THE WORK OF
THE BINDER

7

WARWICK BRO'S & RUTTER

BOOKBINDING DEPARTMENT, FIRST FLOOR

with the pattern required, are clamped in a beam across the ruling-machine and the paper is carried under them by means of a sheet of cloth revolving upon rollers. The color is fed by means of ink-saturated flannel wrapped around the shanks of the pens. By arranging that certain of the pens are fed from flannel carrying one color and others from another, several colors may be ruled simultaneously. In ruling the lines which start from the headline, or from any place other than the edge of the paper, an automatic device called a " gate " is attached to the machine, which permits the paper to feed only at a certain speed, and which causes the pens to be lifted and dropped where required as the paper passes through.

Full Russia Binding with Hub Bands.

After the paper has been ruled, it is carefully examined, and all soiled or broken sheets are either cleaned or removed. It is then sent to be printed, if a heading is required; otherwise, it is folded in sections of four or five sheets according to the thickness and strength of the paper, and placed in a heavy press between boards, to give the book greater solidity. At one time, every part of the work of bookbinding was done by men, but now the folding and sewing are usually done by women. If the book is to be bound by any of the numerous "flat-opening".

9

methods, the manner of the sewing will vary according to the process ; but, in the ordinary book, the sheets are sewn with linen cord or thread on strips of strong tape or vellum. The strength and durability of a book depend on the sewing more than on any other one thing that enters into the making, and the greatest care must be exercised that only the best materials are used, and that every sheet is securely fastened. The strips to which the sections are sewn are the hinges upon which they open, and which unite the book to its cover. The end papers, which are made separately, are sewn in with the book, and are important elements in its strength and wearing qualities.

FOLDING AND SEWING

The book is now trimmed and the edges are stained or marbled. Every blank book of any size should be marbled, for, next to gild-ing—which, of course, is never applied to a blank book—no finishing for book edges is so generally satisfactory. Marbling is done by dipping the edges of the book into a liquid size of gum tragacanth, upon the surface of which colors have been thrown and formed into a design. A good marbler is a rarity even in large binderies. He is not an ordinary artisan —he is an accomplished man among his fellows. He throws his colors, not at haphazard, but with an eye to the final effect, and he arranges and combs them with the dexterity of an artist. As each design will stand but one dipping great care is essential to get a uniform pattern every edge.

MARBLING

The sections of the book are now glued along the back to unite them to one another and to prevent them from working loose. The back is then rounded with a hammer to give it shape and to hold the spring-back which is afterwards added, and the book is again placed in the press to set, that it may retain the shape now finally given it. Although apparently trifling, these are all important details. The first requirement of all blank-books is strength ; appearance comes afterwards. Cheap thread, inferior glue, imperfect rounding, neglect or carelessness in any of a score of little things, may destroy the finest product of a bookbinder's skill.

The book is now lined along the back with strong canvas and bands of leather are drawn over the edges, forming, with the outside sheets of the book, which are folded back to about three inches in width, what are known as the " lugs," to which the sides are secured. The boards for the sides are now added. The thickness of the boards depends altogether on the size and weight of the book, and must be of the best quality of millboard so as not to warp or break. The spring-back which encircles the back of the book, and to which the leather covering is pasted, must be of the best tarboard. This back is intended to assist in throwing open the book at any place so as to leave a surface flat enough to allow of writing close into the crease, and is made to grip the edges of the book snugly. The boards forming the sides are split at the edges nearest the back and the lugs inserted to make the hinge and fasten the book

11

WARWICK BRO'S & RUTTER

PRINTING DEPARTMENT COMPOSING ROOM

to its cover. The raised hub-bands on the back are made by fastening strips of strawboard across the hack, forming it into panels. On ordinary bindings the panels are five in number, with the bottom one a trifle longer than t' e others. This rule, however, may be varied to suit the style of binding.

The book is now ready for the outer covering. The finest blank-books are bound in full Calf with Russia bands, but without hubs, or in full Russia with hubs. Cheaper styles are half Calf, half Russia, or half Sheep, all having cloth sides, or full Canvas with Russia bands. Care must be exercised that the leather is cut along the grain in orde: that it will stretch well. After being cut to the required size and the edges pared, it is dampened to soften it and to make it stretch, pasted on the inside and then drawn tightly over the back and sides of the book and fastened. It is first stretched well over the hack, rubbed in at the sides of the hubs so that they stand out as though cut from leather, pressed in at the hinges to allow free play to the sides, turned in at the head and tail and smoothed well

LEATHER COVERING

Russia Binding with single Russia Bands and Corners.

over all. Slight rods of wood or thick cords are then fitted into the joints of the hinges and the book is put into the press for a short time. When taken out the Russia bands, or cloth sides if a half-bound book, or other details are added. The end papers are then glued down and the book is again placed in the press to set. It should now remain undisturbed for several days to dry and season.

13

A blank-book when first removed from the press is hard and unyielding. The first duty of the finisher is to " ease " and soften the back to allow it to open freely. He then makes and **LETTERING AND FINISHING** puts on the titles and any other ornamentation that he may see fit. The upper title, in the second panel from the head, usually indicates the name or character of the book, and the lower one, in the fourth panel, the name or initials of the owner. Blank-books should have as little gold finishing as possible, and the lettering should be brief and readable. An ornamental roll in black ink on a Calf binding, or in gold on a Russia binding, is usually run around the edge and a line or two put on the hubs and bands on the back.

The loose canvas, basil or moleskin cover is added after the book is made. All well-bound books should be fitted with a loose cover in order to preserve the binding. The cost is comparatively trifling, and when the book is put away for reference and the cover removed, the binding remains clean and perfect. In many cases the loose cover is intended to be **LOOSE COVERS** permanent, and the titles are put on it rather than on the book within. These covers are often made with protecting leather bands and corners to give them strength and durability.

Inventive minds have been engaged for many years in trying to devise some process of sewing or binding that will permit blank-books to open perfectly flat. Several methods have been found

Full Calf Binding with double Russia Bands and Ends.

14

that in some measure seemed to meet the requirements, but only at the sacrifice of much of the strength of the book. To preserve this and at the same time to secure the necessary free- FLAT-OPENING BOOKS dom of opening was the difficulty. This at last has been overcome, and the largest blank-books are now bound by Messrs. Warwick Bro's & Rutter by a process that not only ensures a satisfactory flat opening, but at the same time adds strength and firmness to the binding. Al- though the invention is covered by patent, its use adds but an insignificant amount to the cost of the book.

A newly made blank-book should be handled with care. The sewing, gluing and moving are likely to be hard and in- flexible, and the spring-back, which is full of life and vitality, holds the edges with a firm grip. To force the book open at the centre will likely result in breaking the back or impairing the sewing. The glory of the book is its strength, and opening and closing it violently or carelessly may cause serious injury to its strength and wearing qualities. A new book should be placed on it on the desk, and, TO OPEN A BLANK-BOOK after throwing back the cover, a few leaves should be lifted at a time until the desired page is reached. It should be closed in the same manner. A blank-book at all times should receive careful treatment, for it is one of the highest products of the artisans' skill.

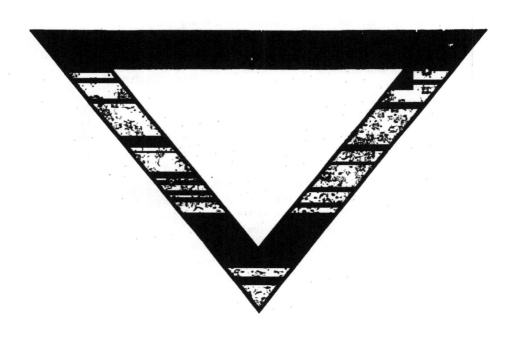